for all curious creative children, who bring a world of colors and joy to our lives. may each page of this book inspire you to explore your imagination and express all your vivacity. may the magic of colors accompany you on all your adventures. have fun coloring and let your minds fly free

with love and joy
Aunt Alê. 2024

ACMℂ
Ales'miranda publications

Test color page

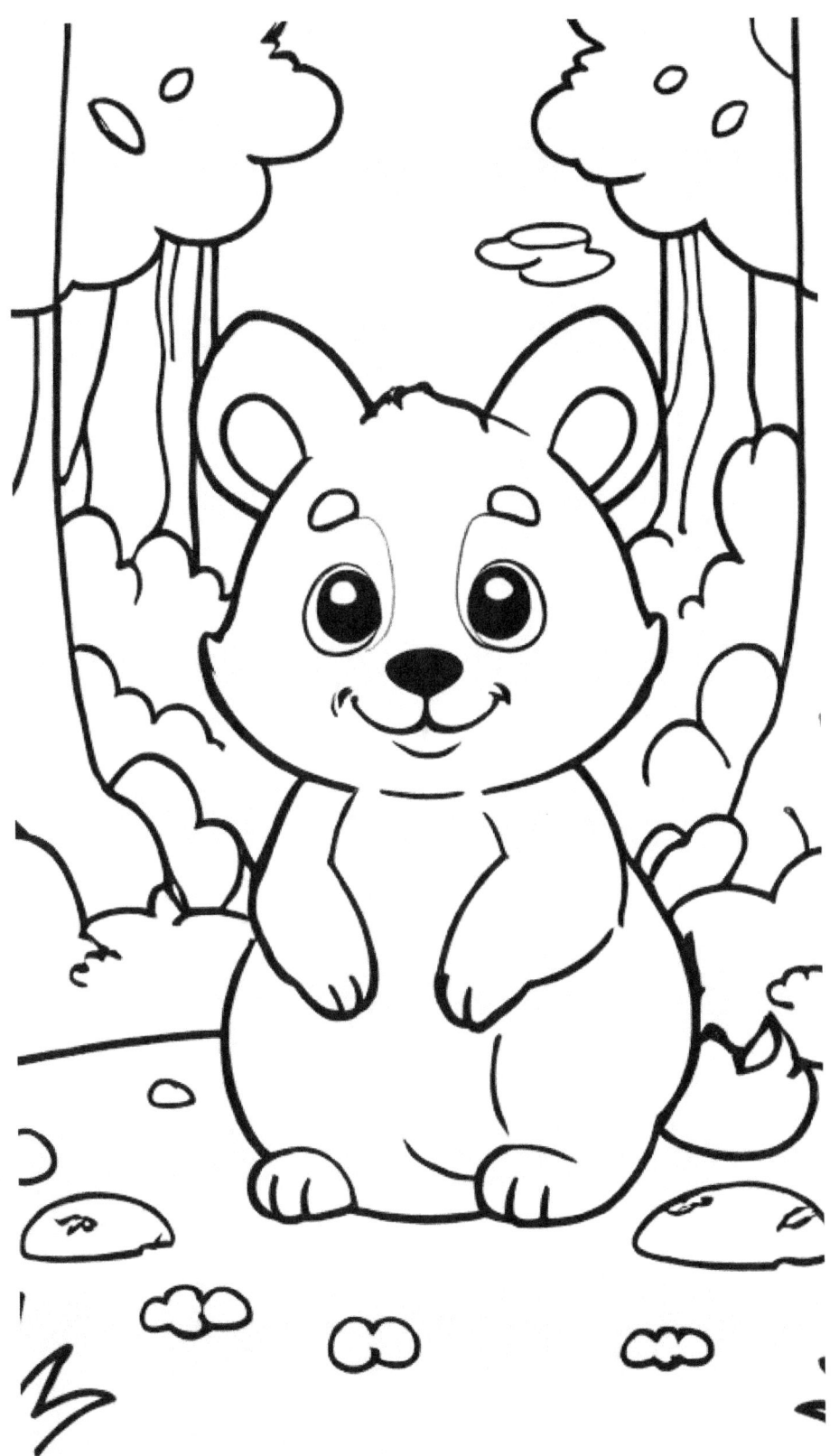

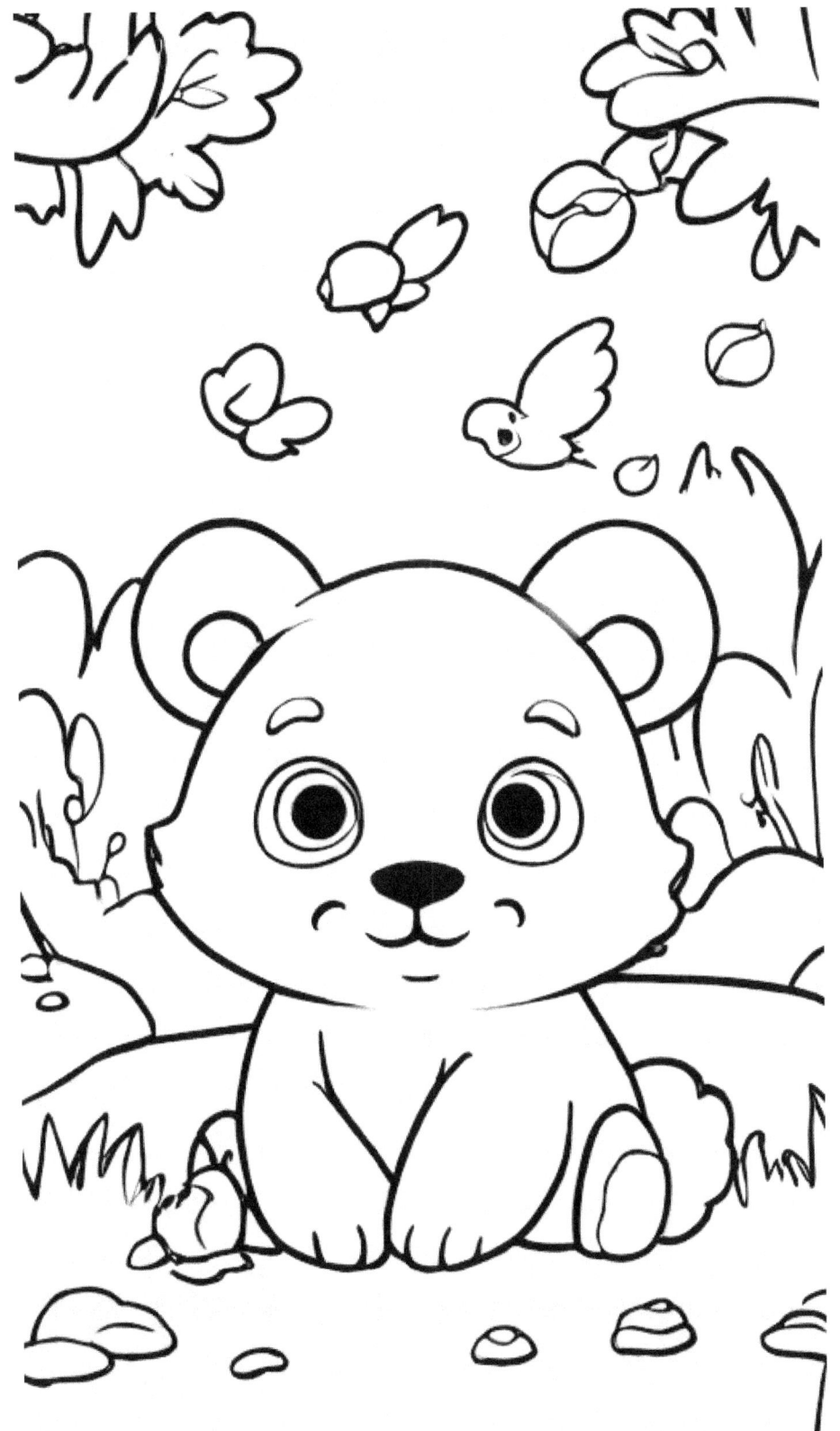

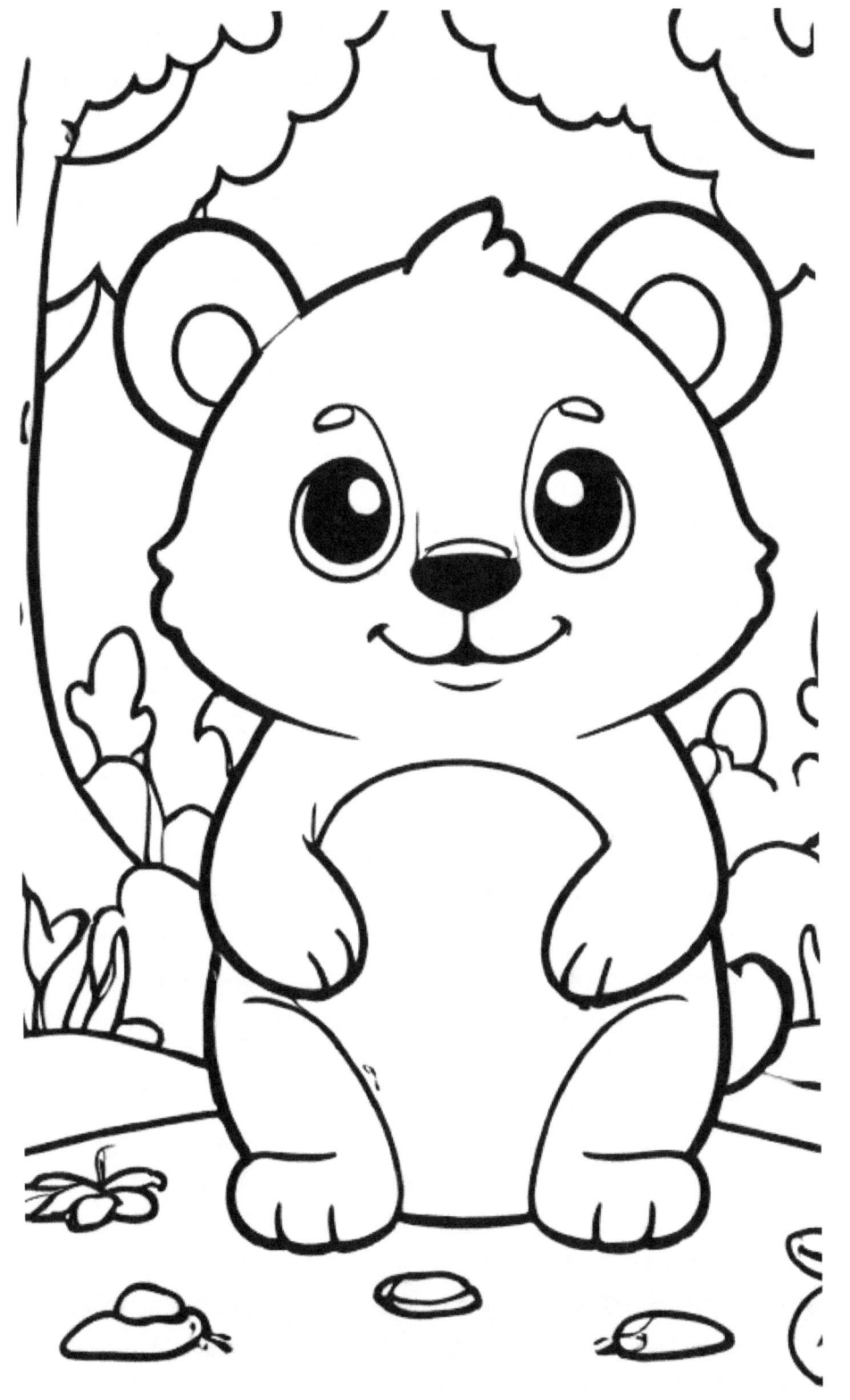

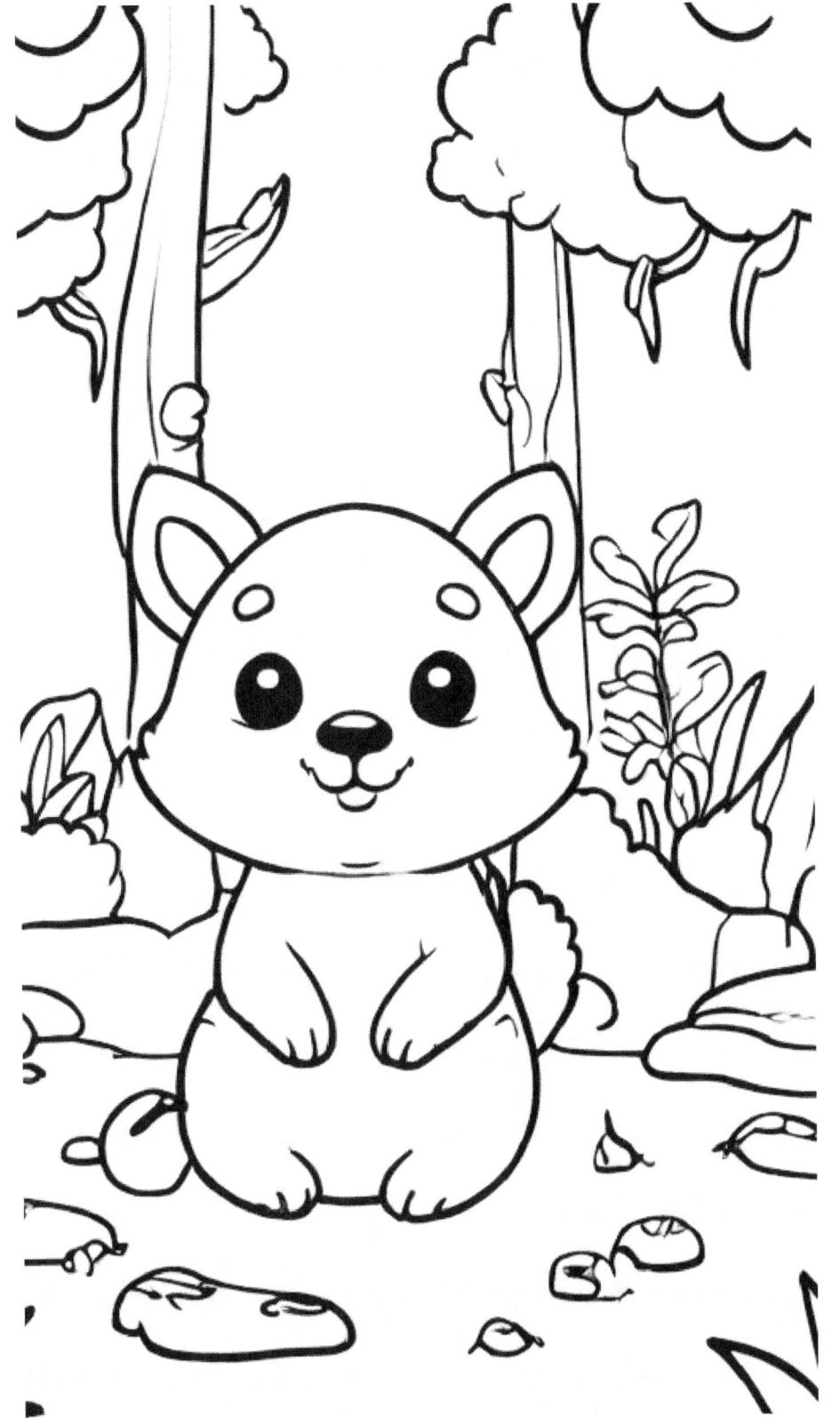

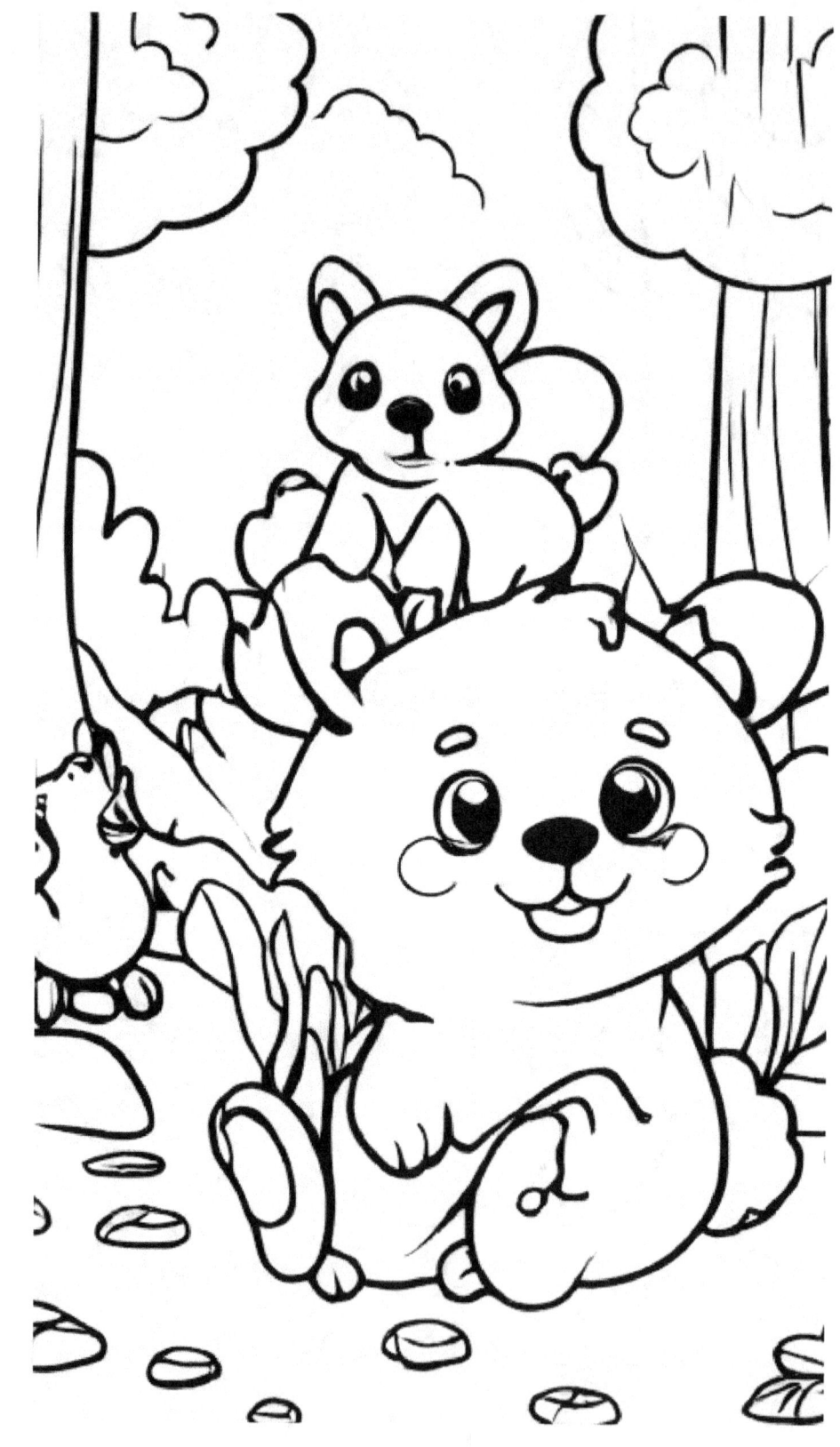

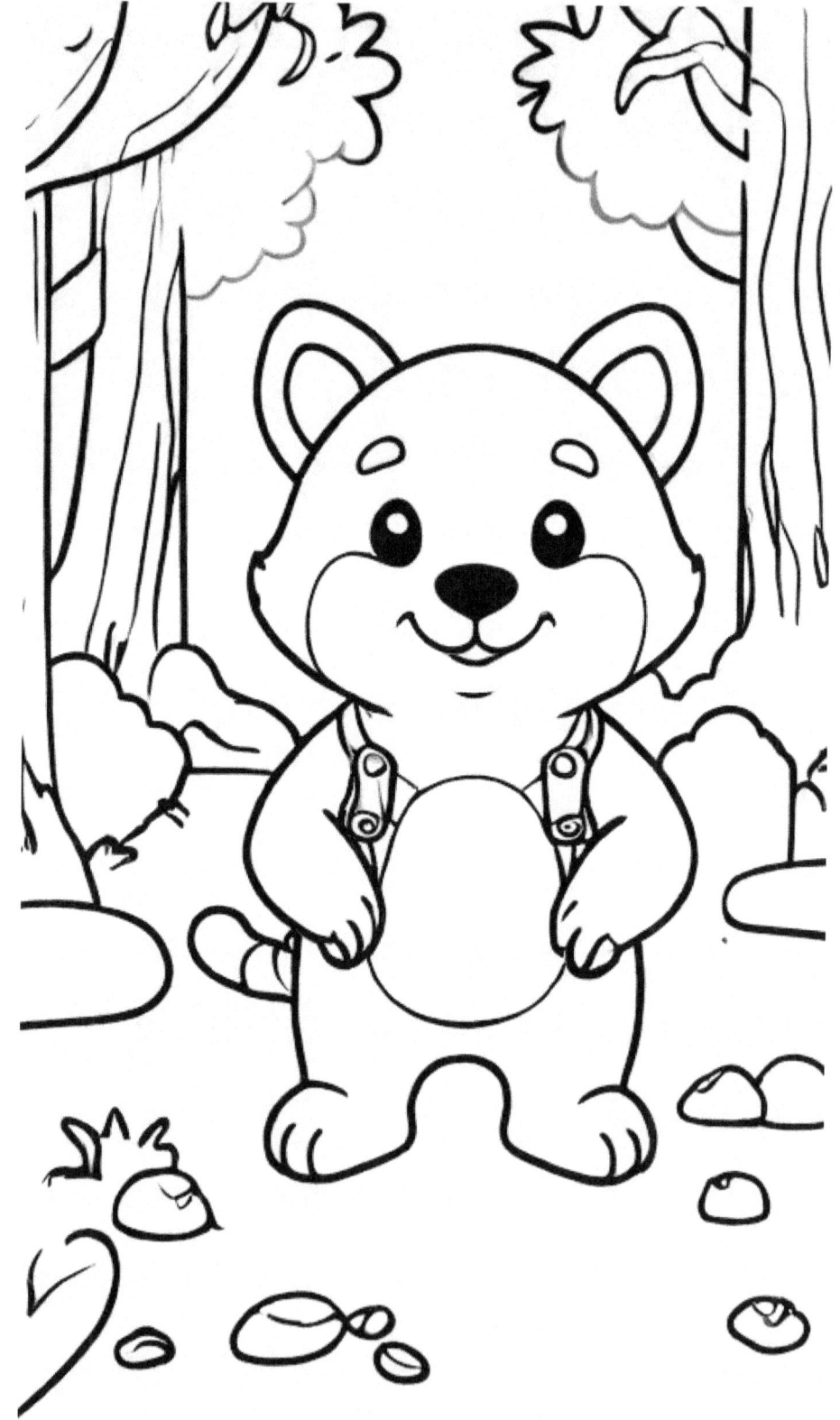

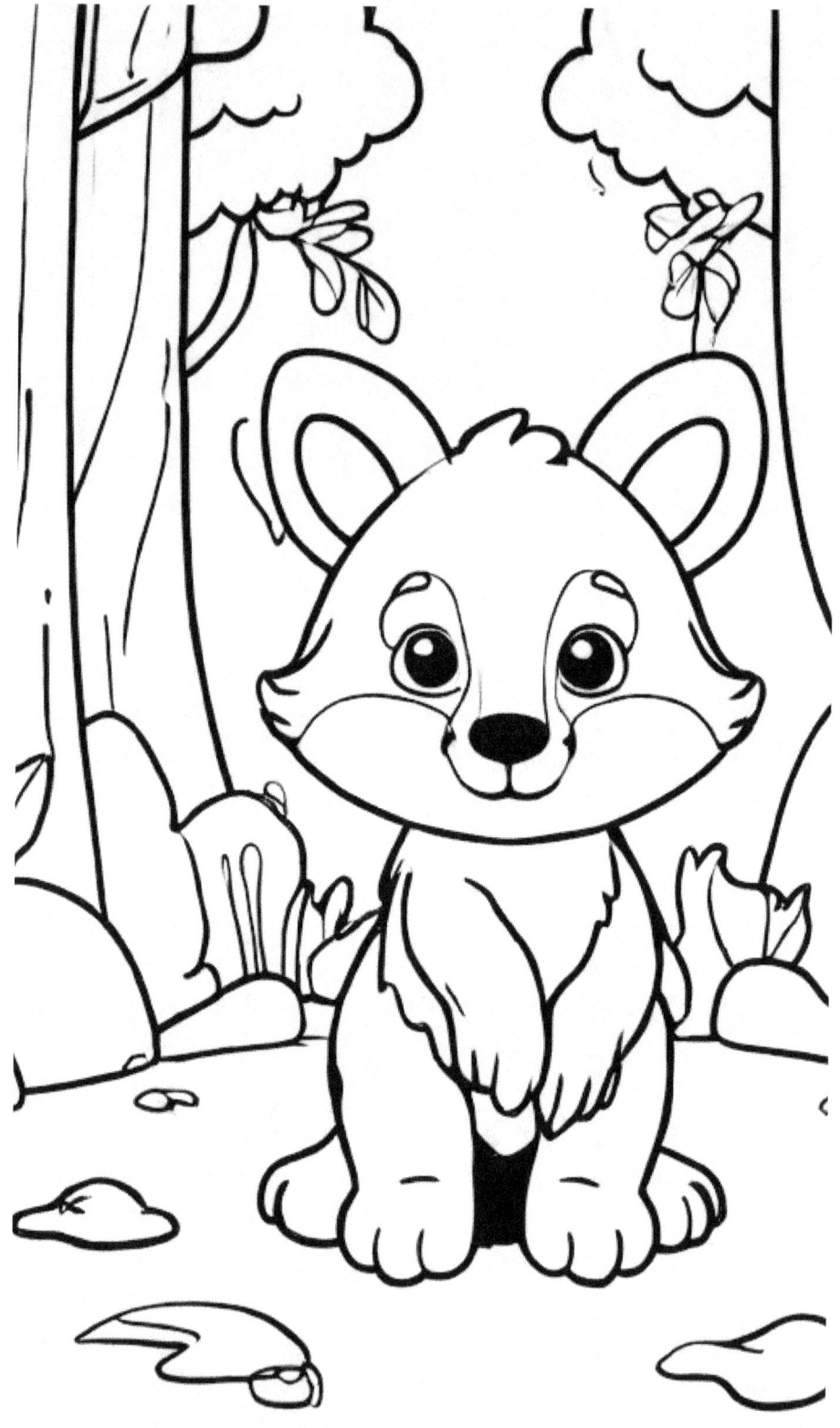

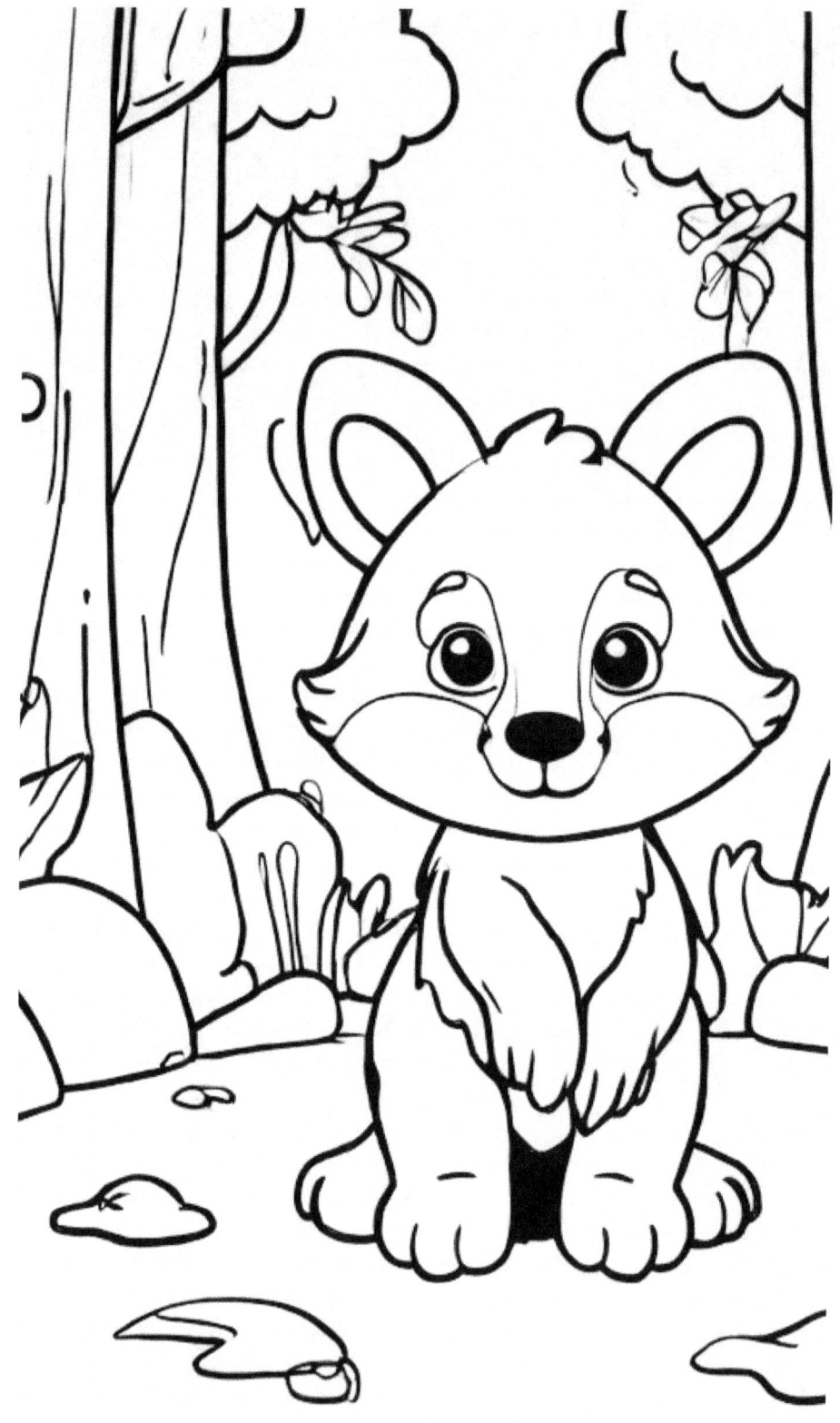

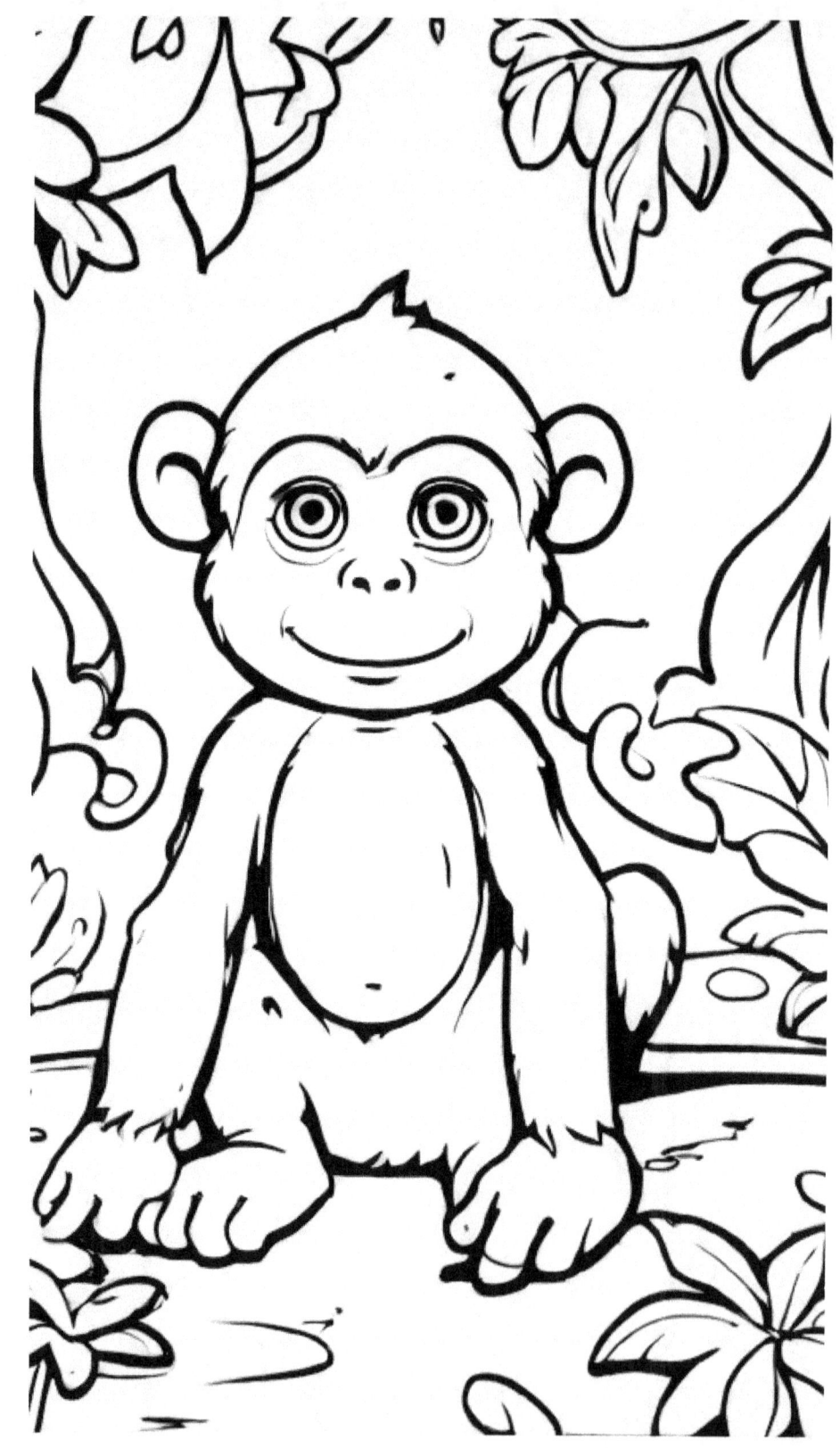

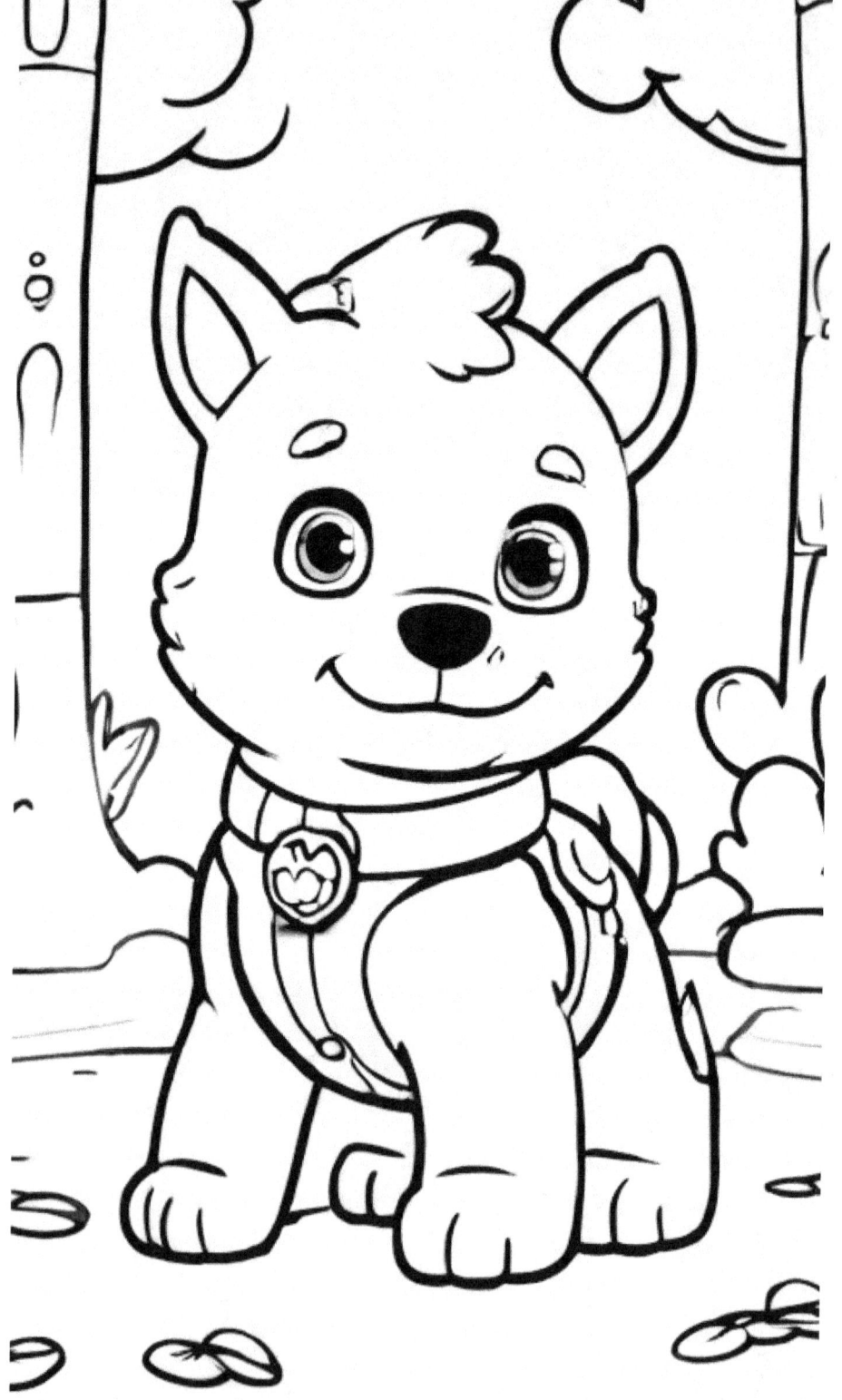

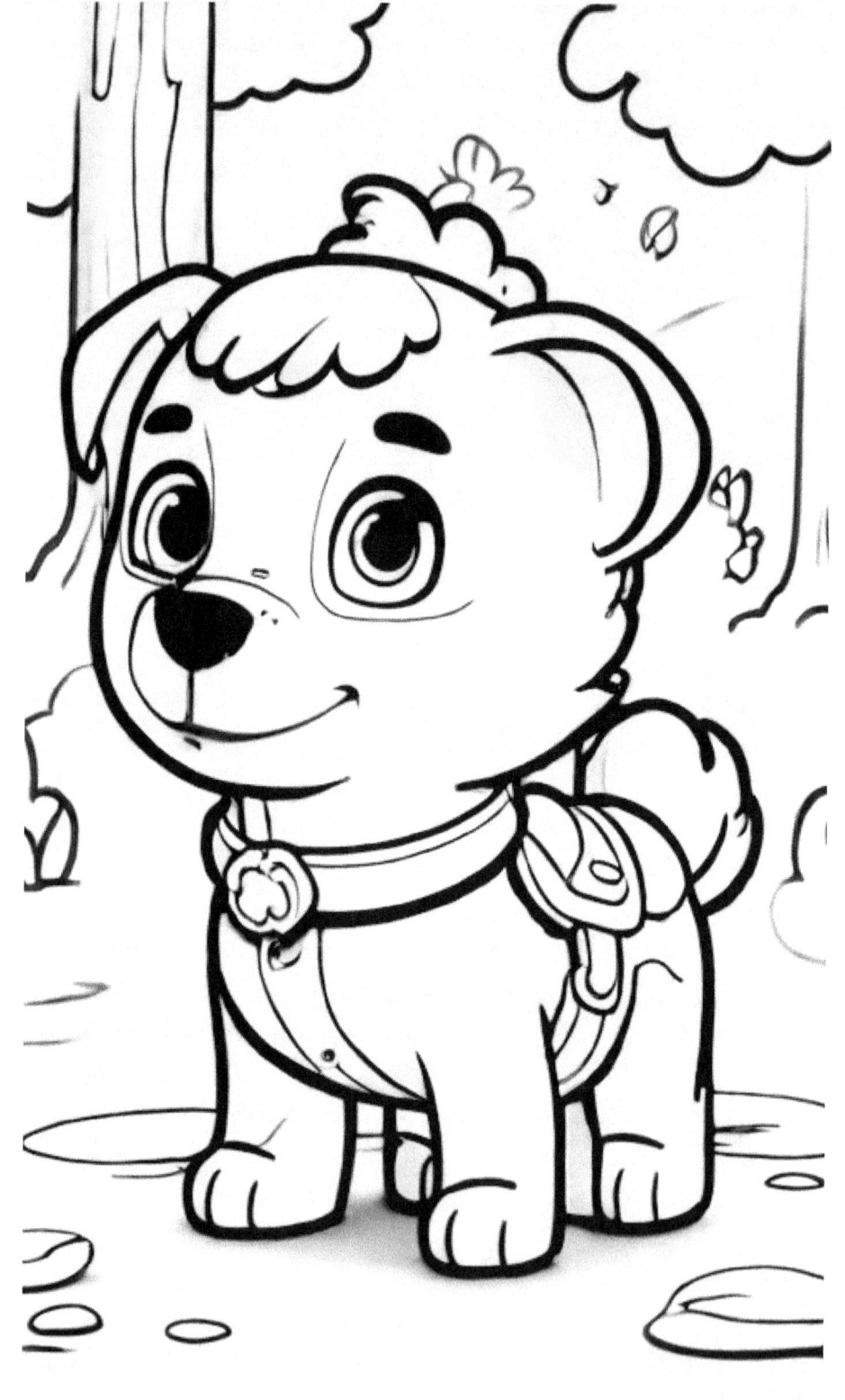

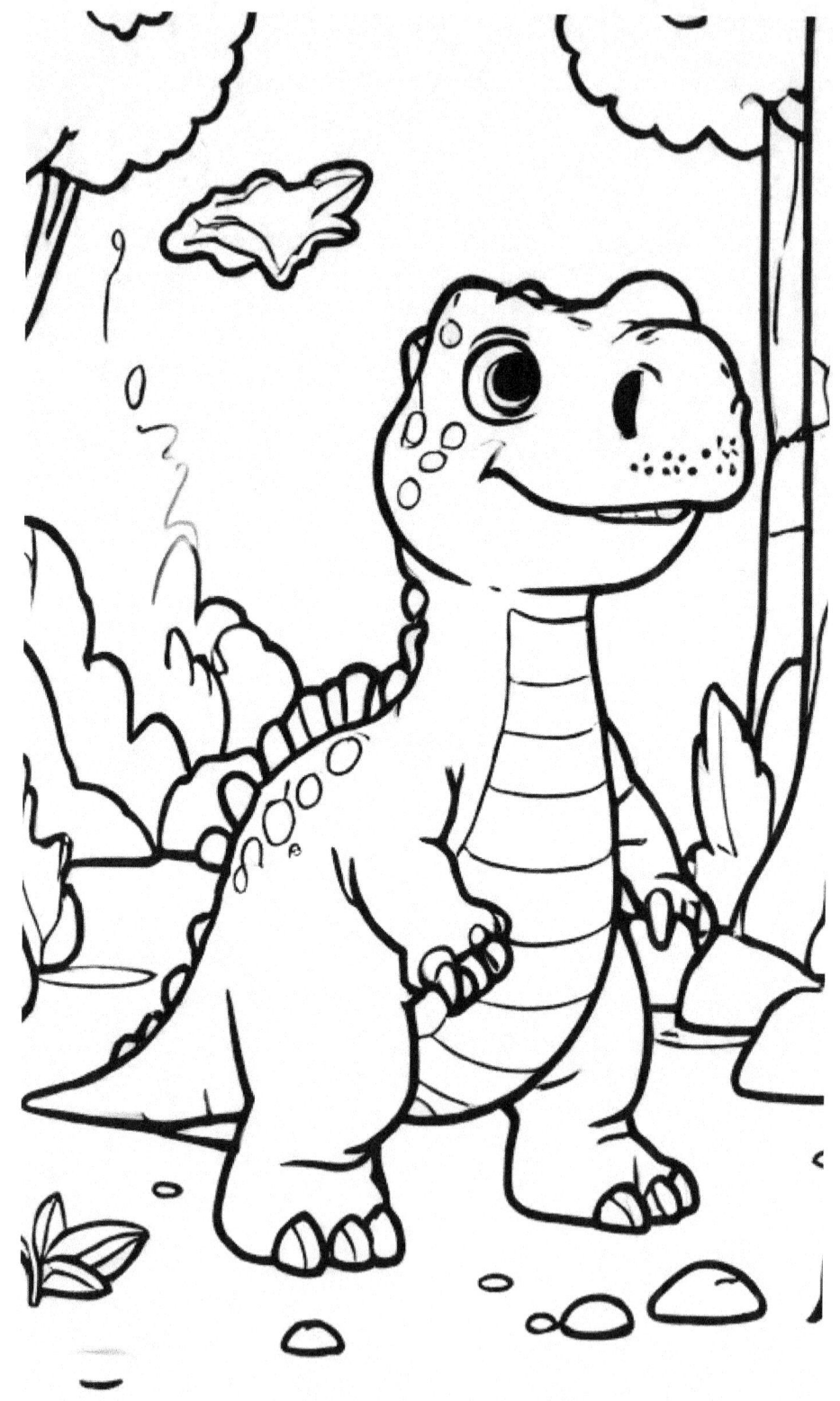

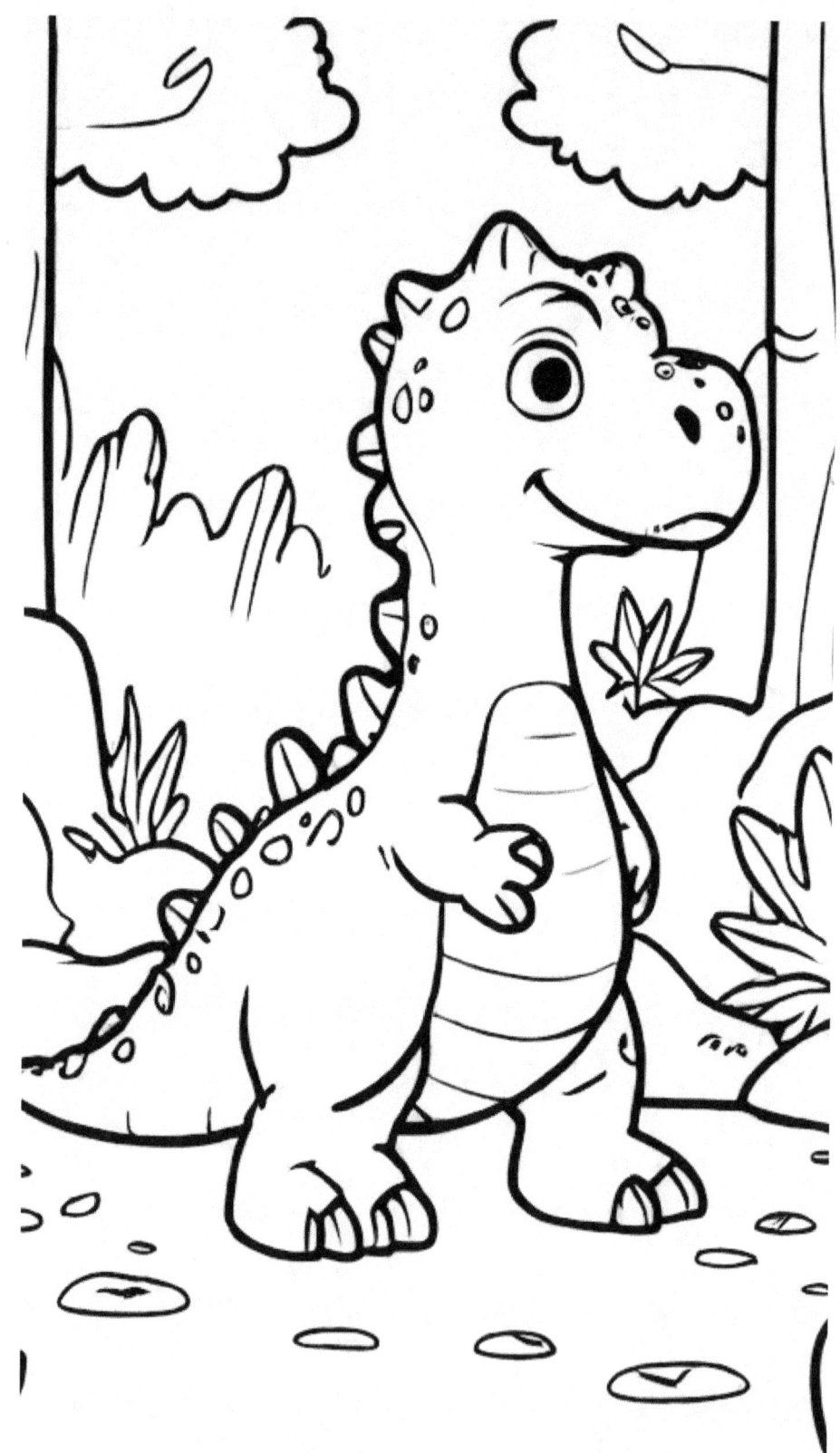

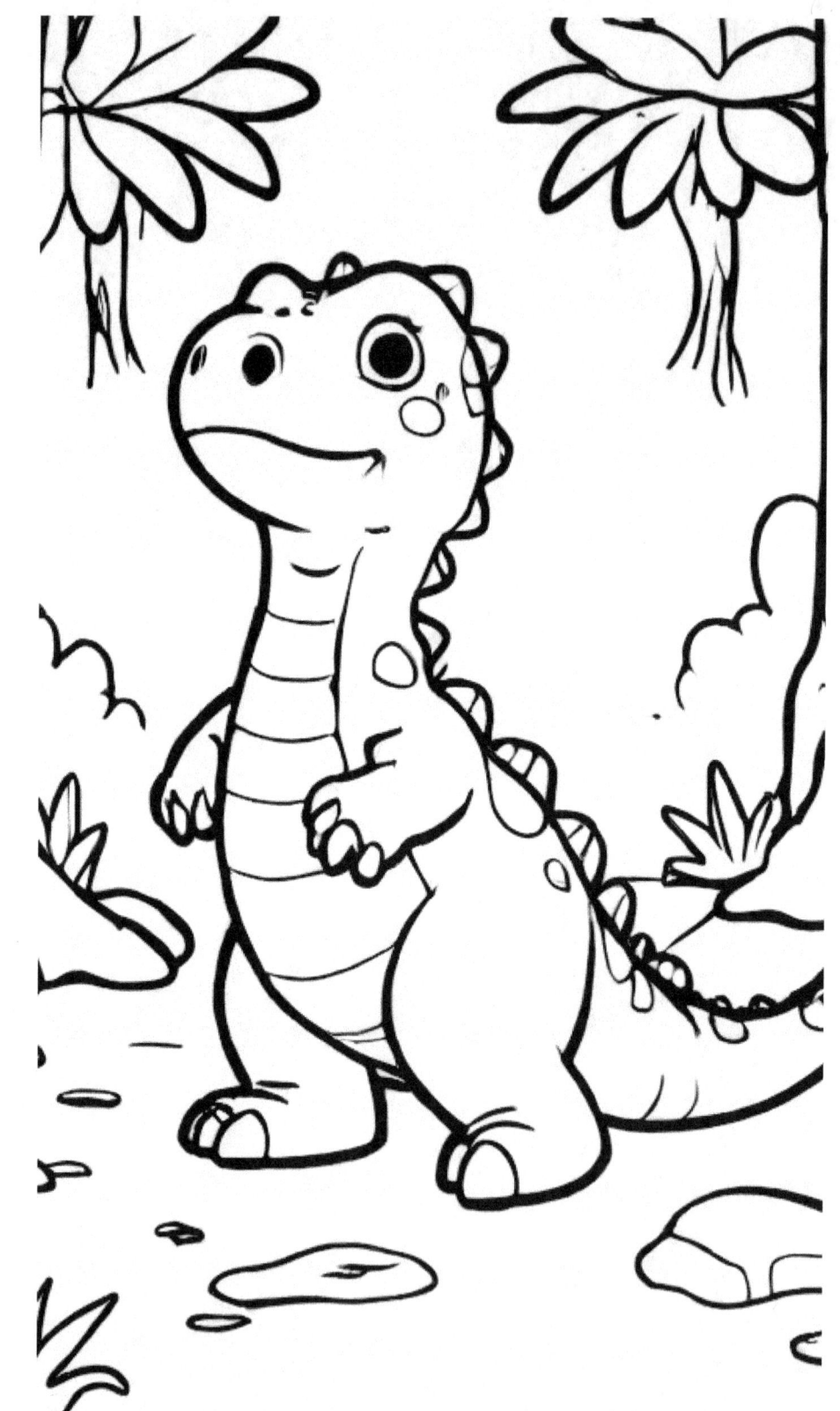

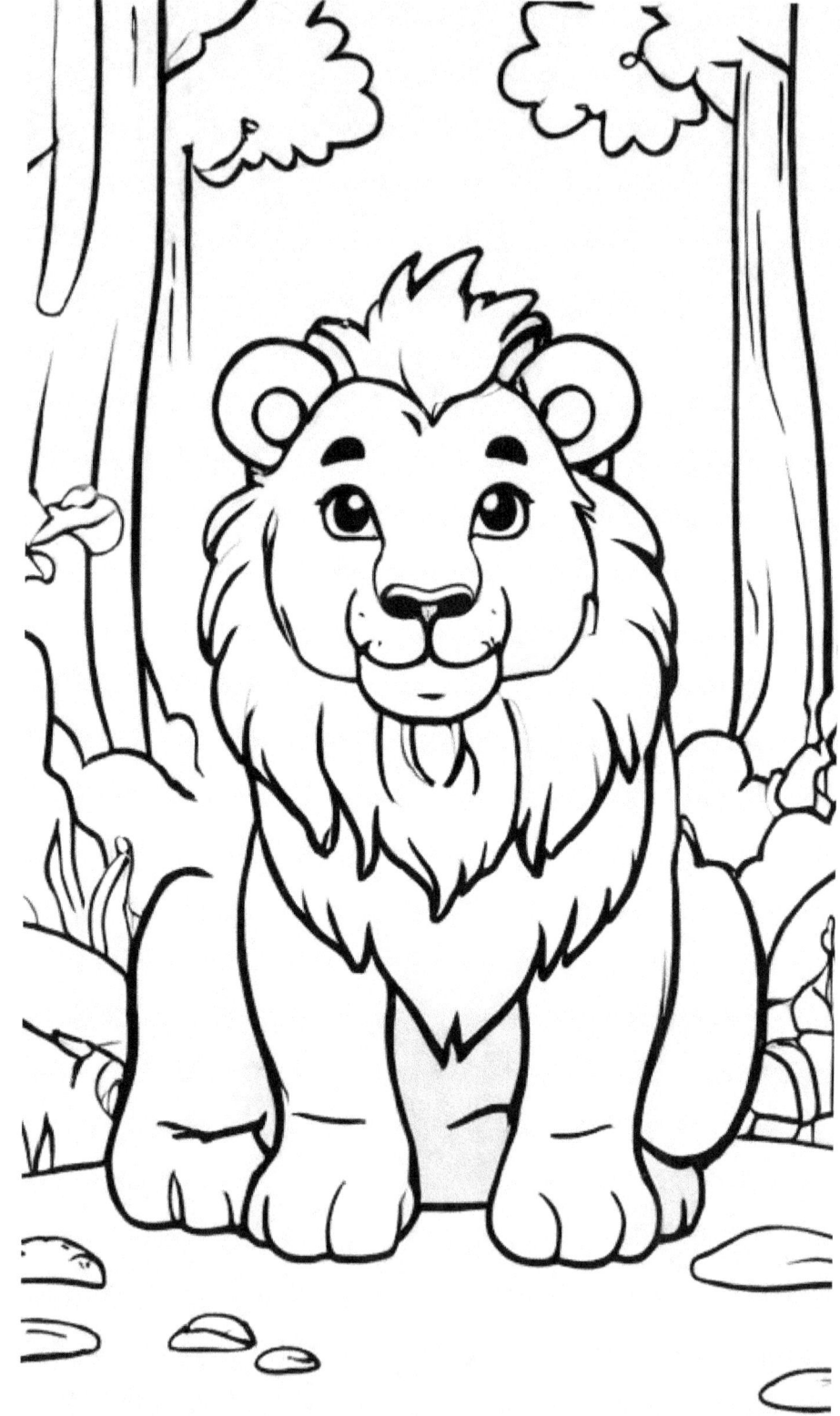

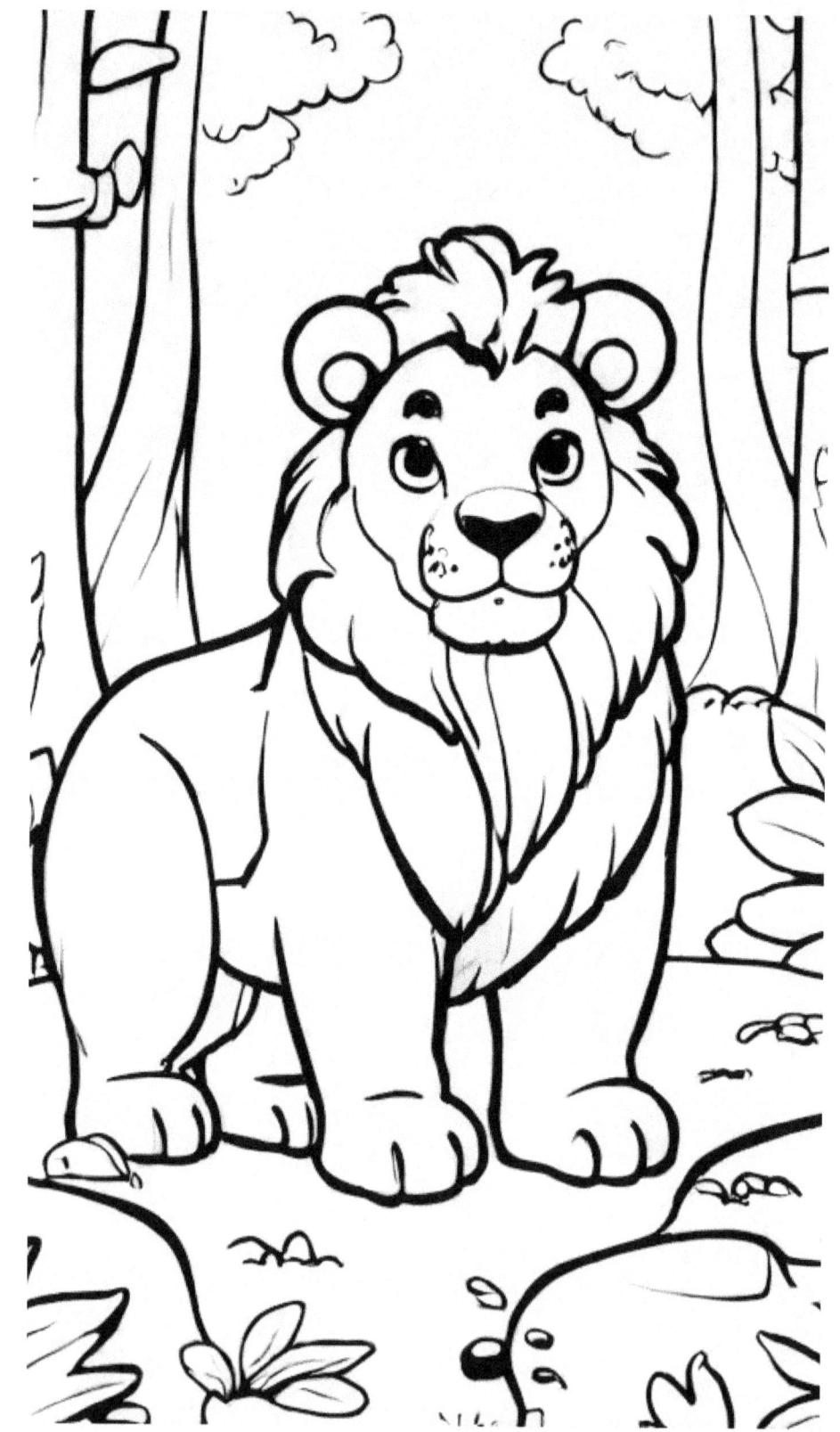

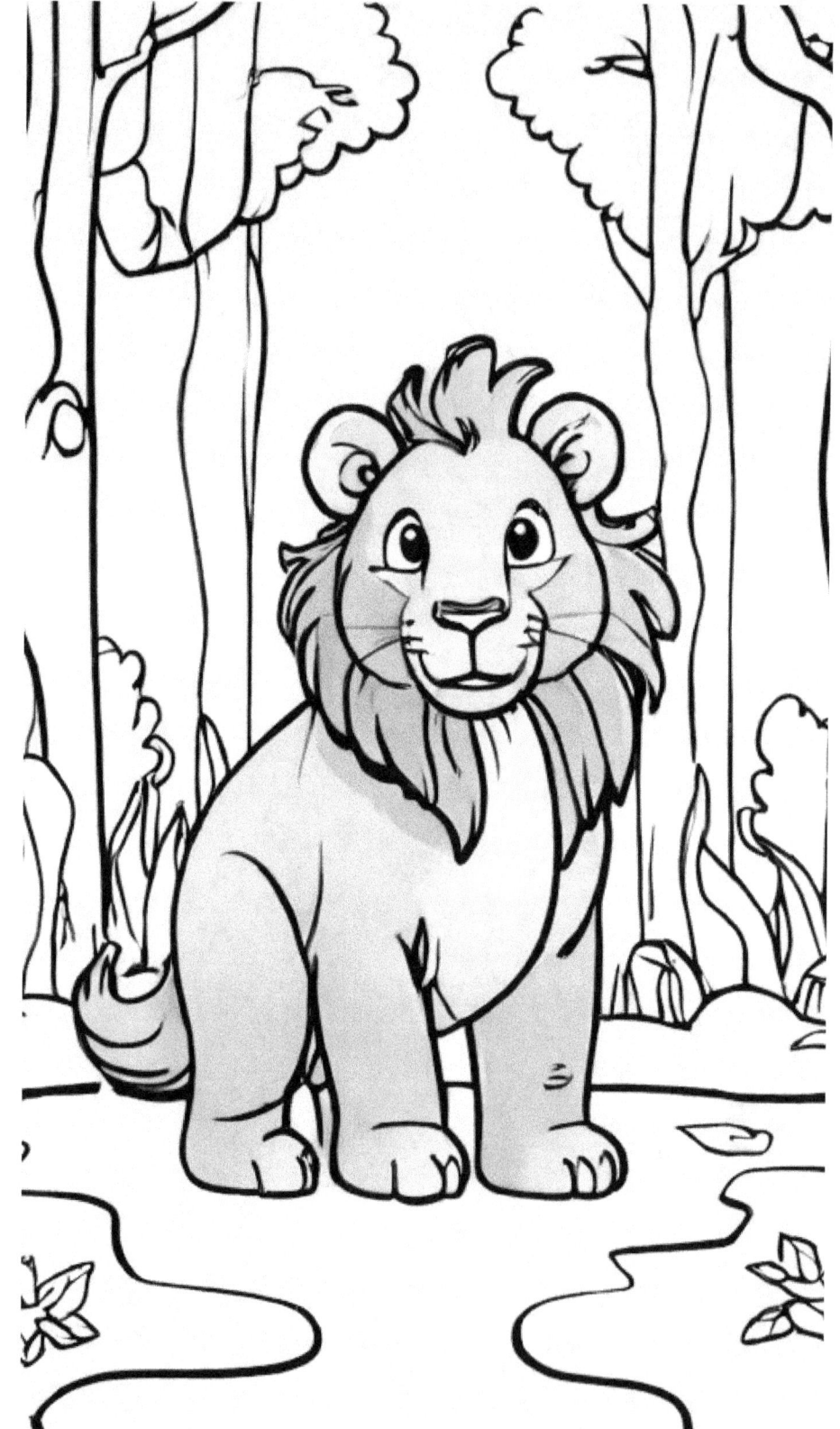

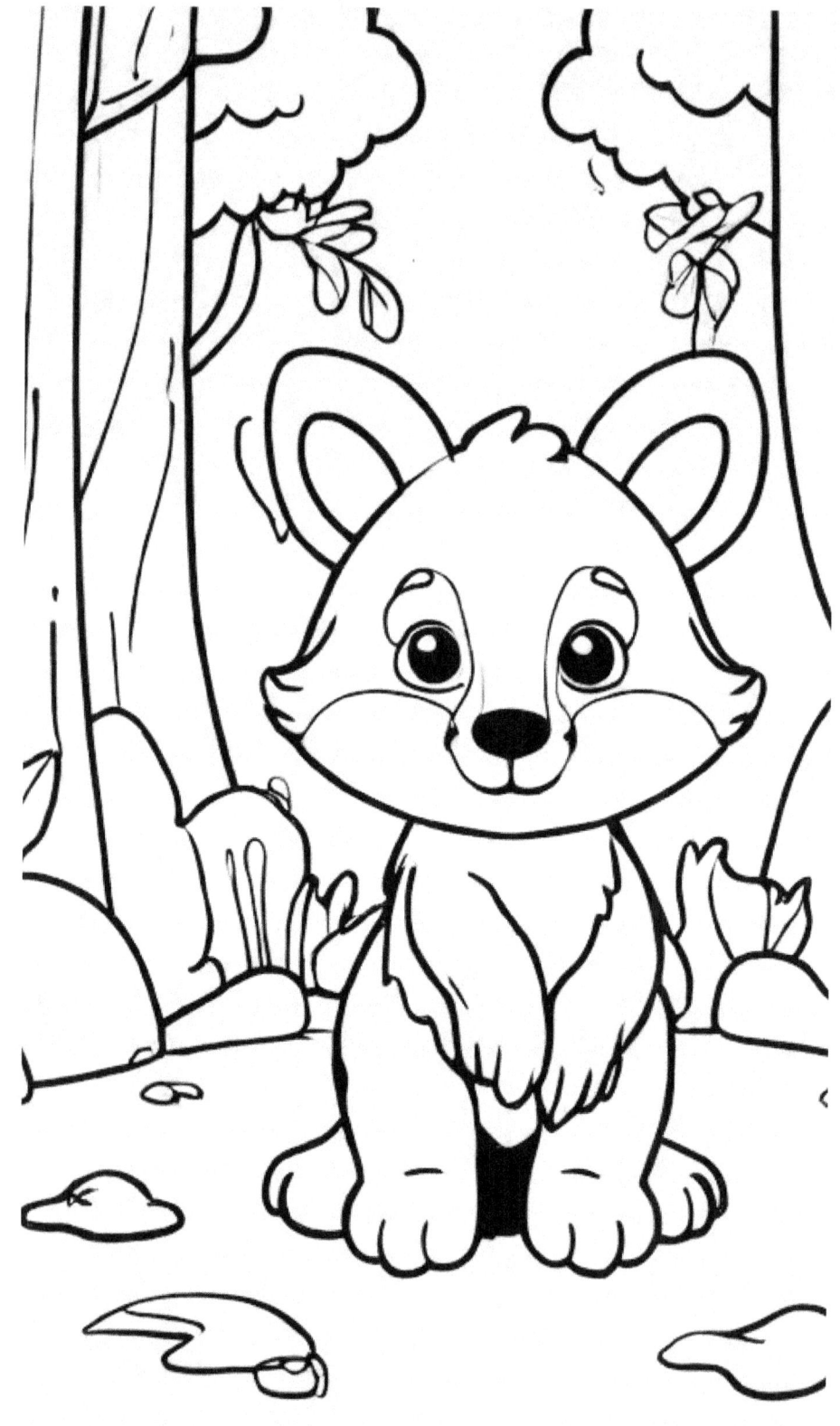

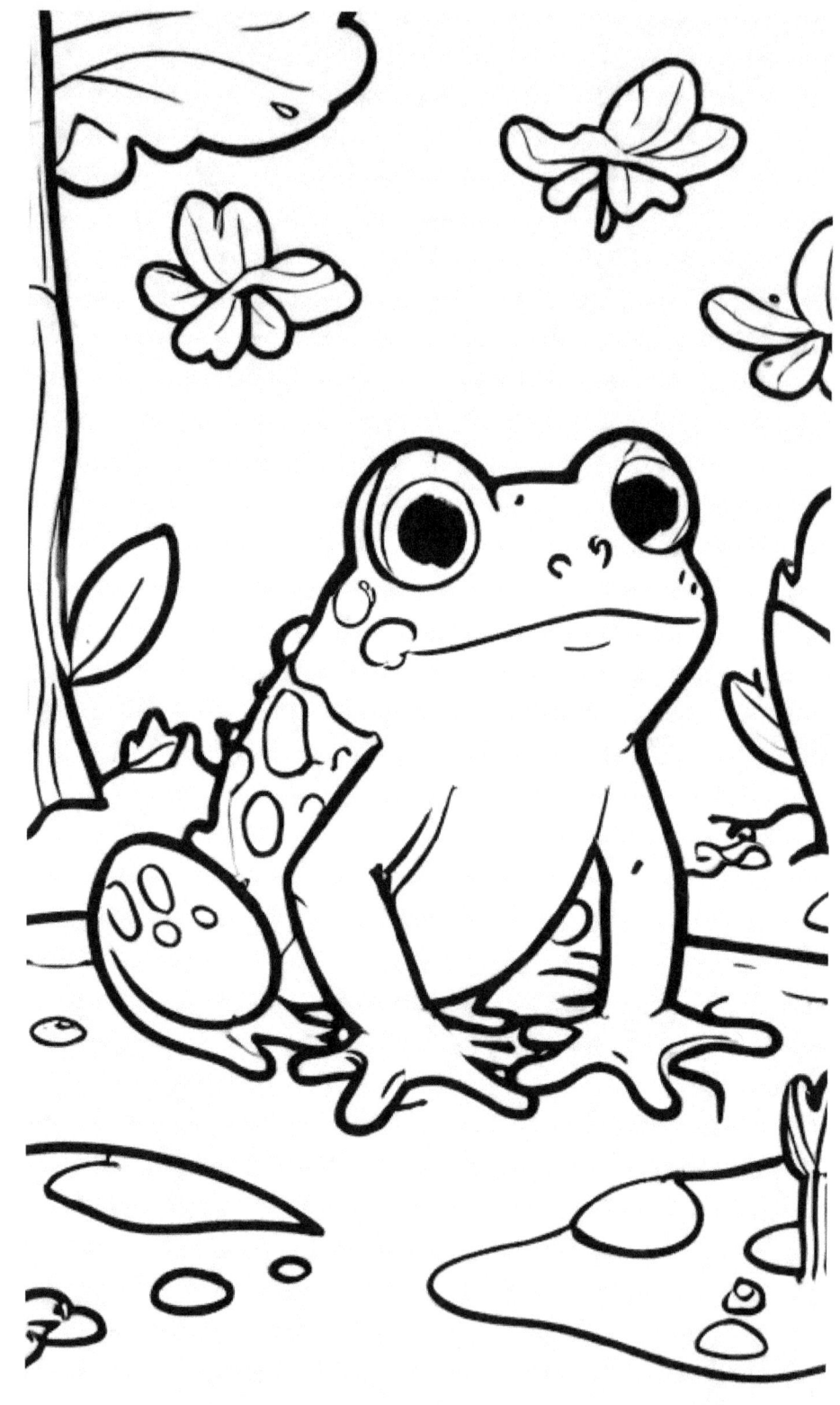

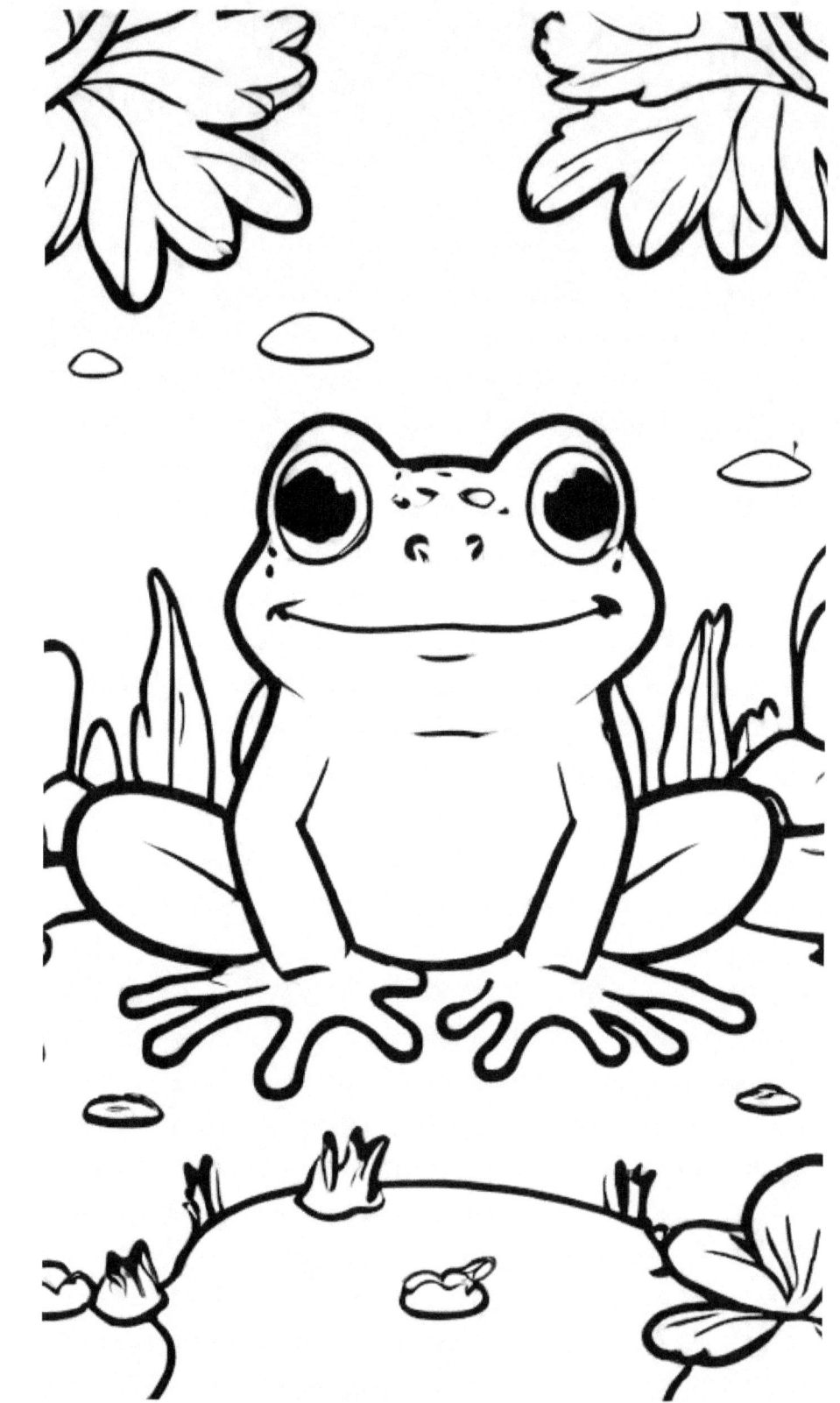

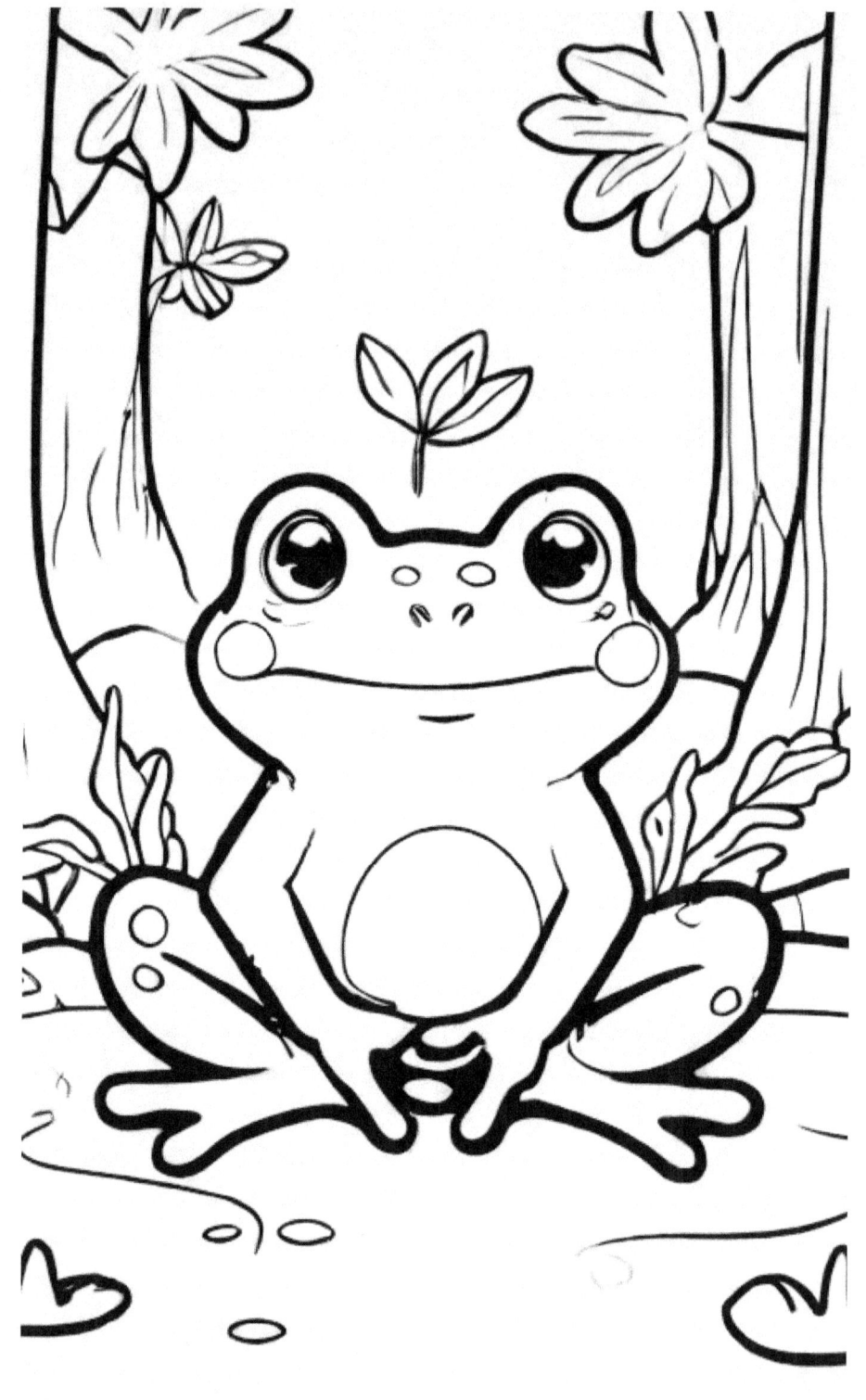

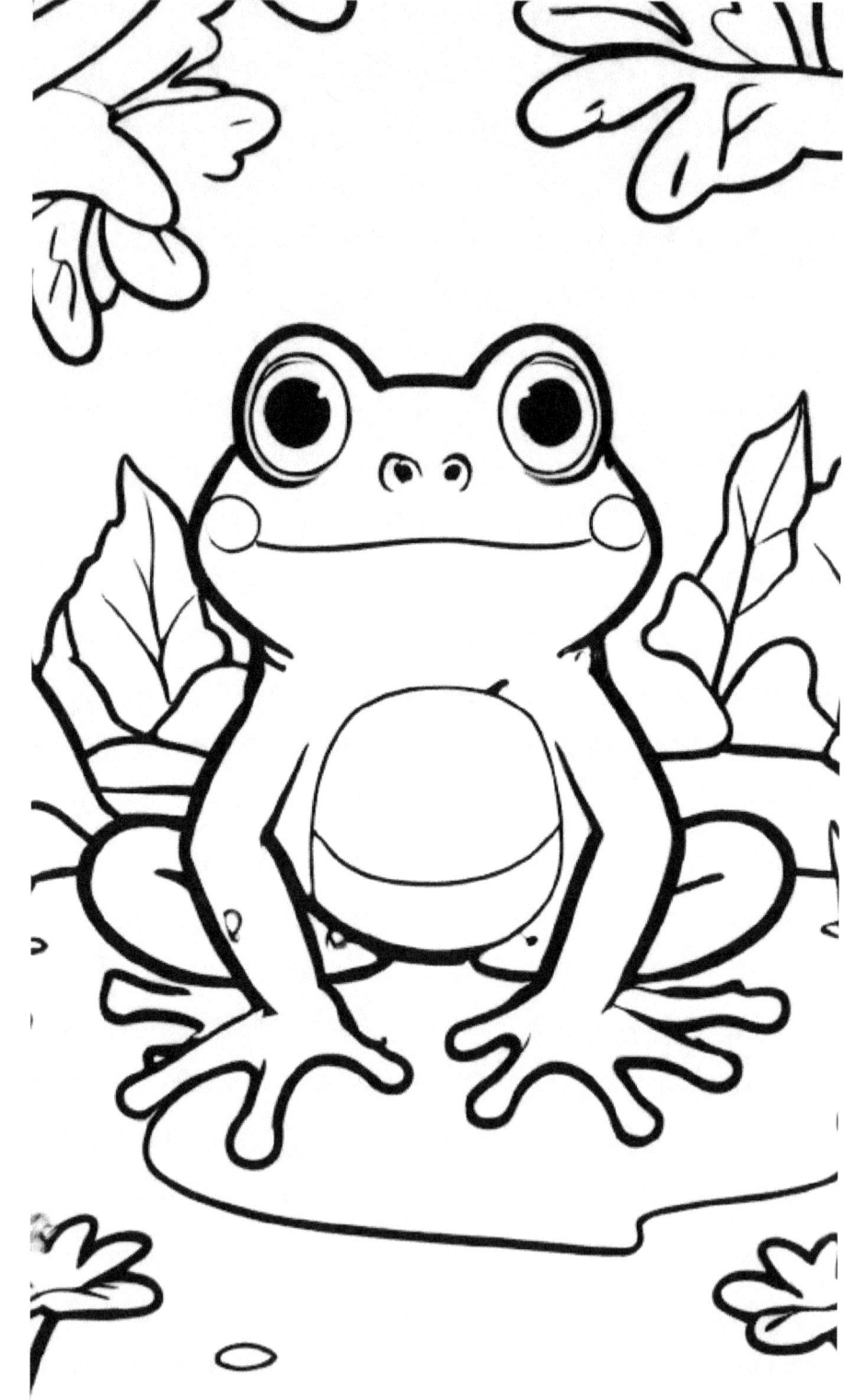

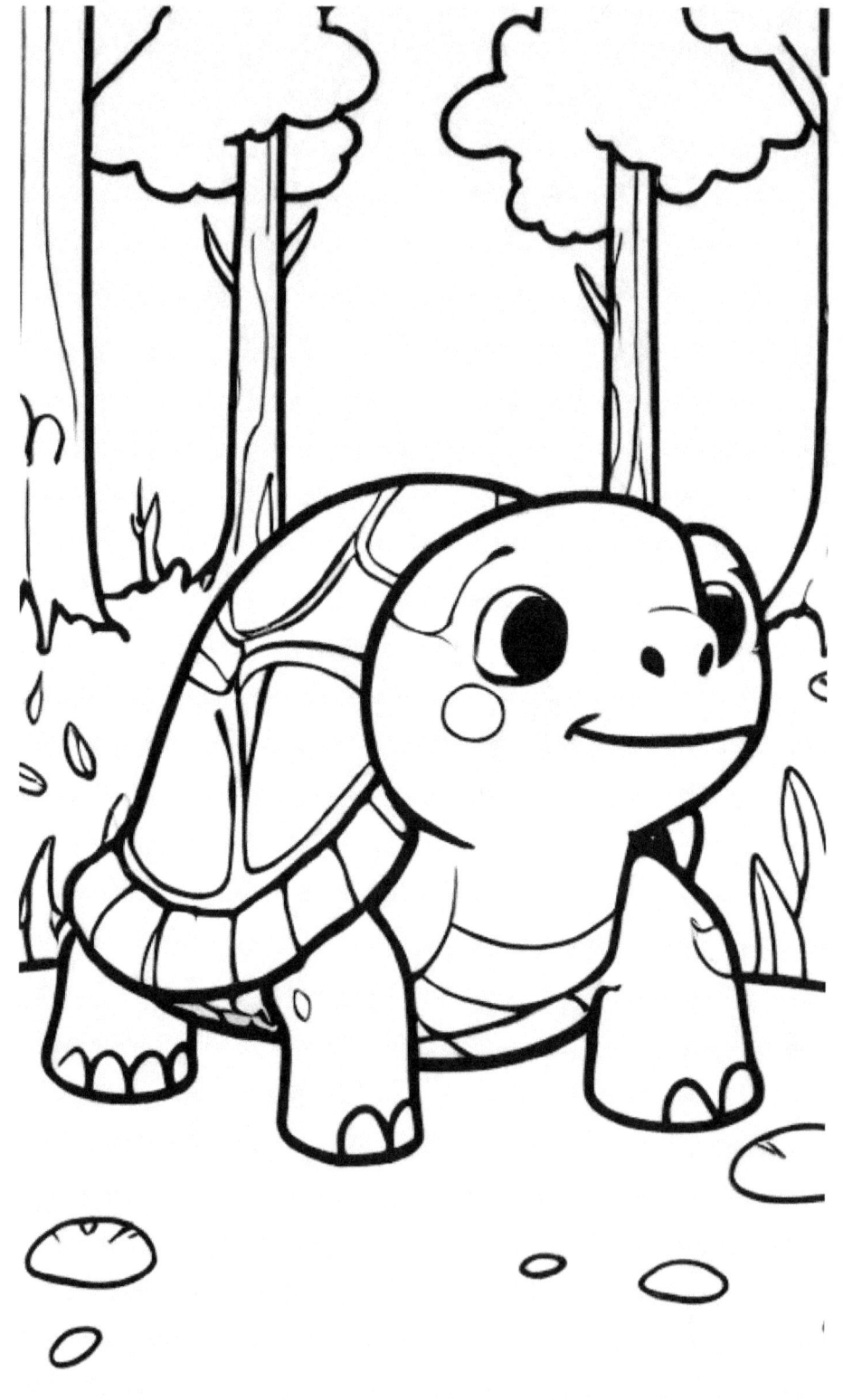

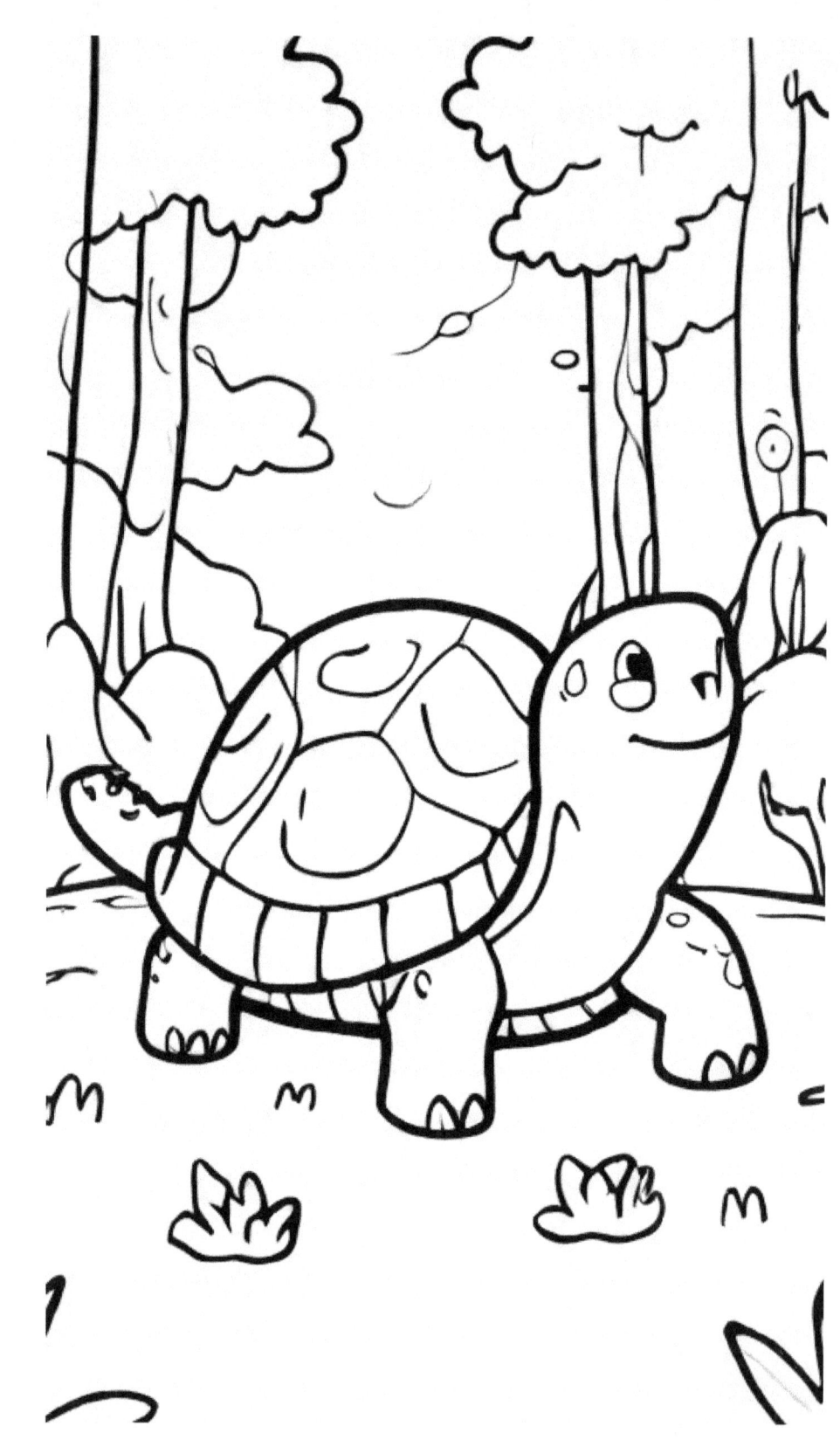

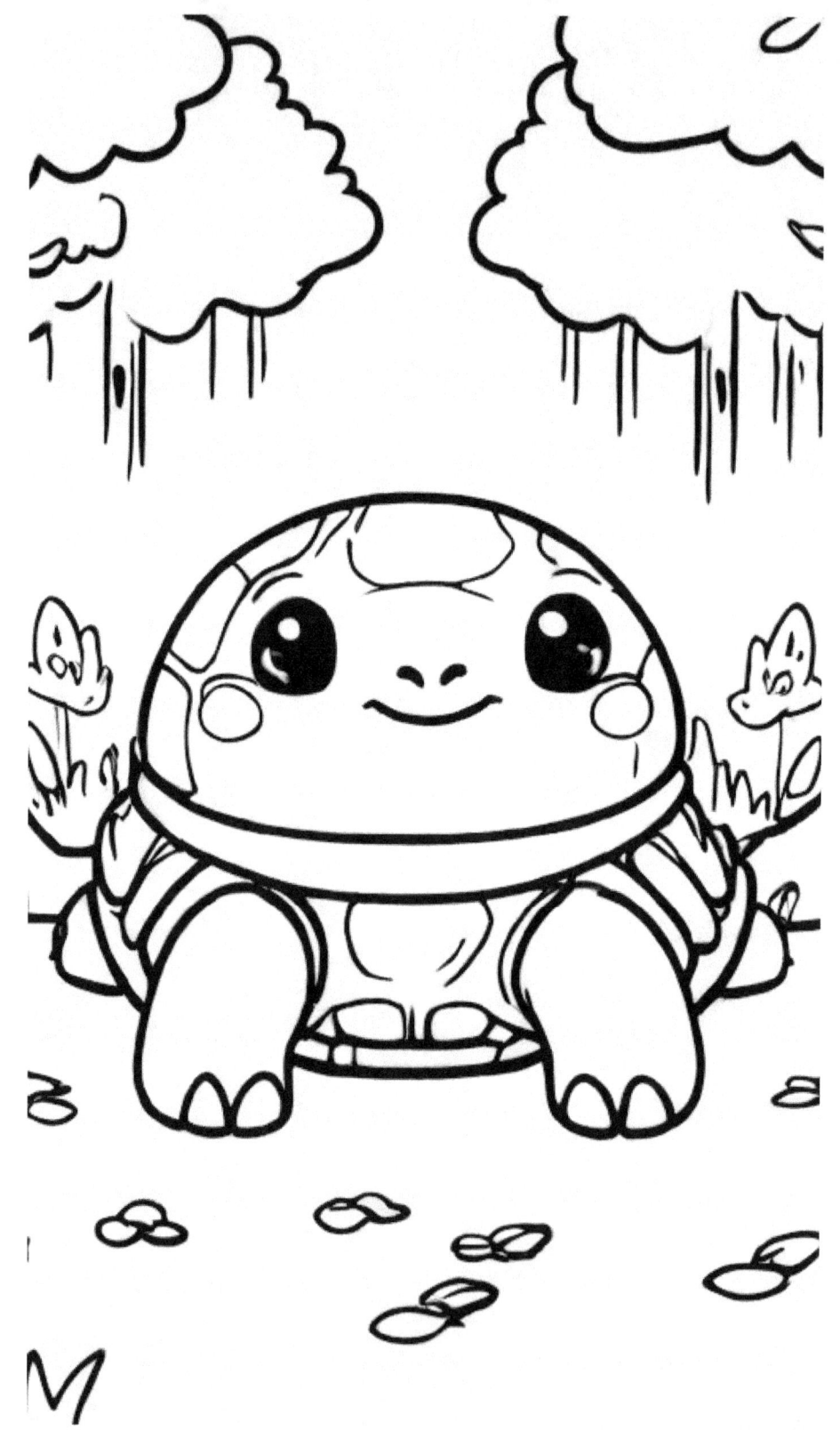

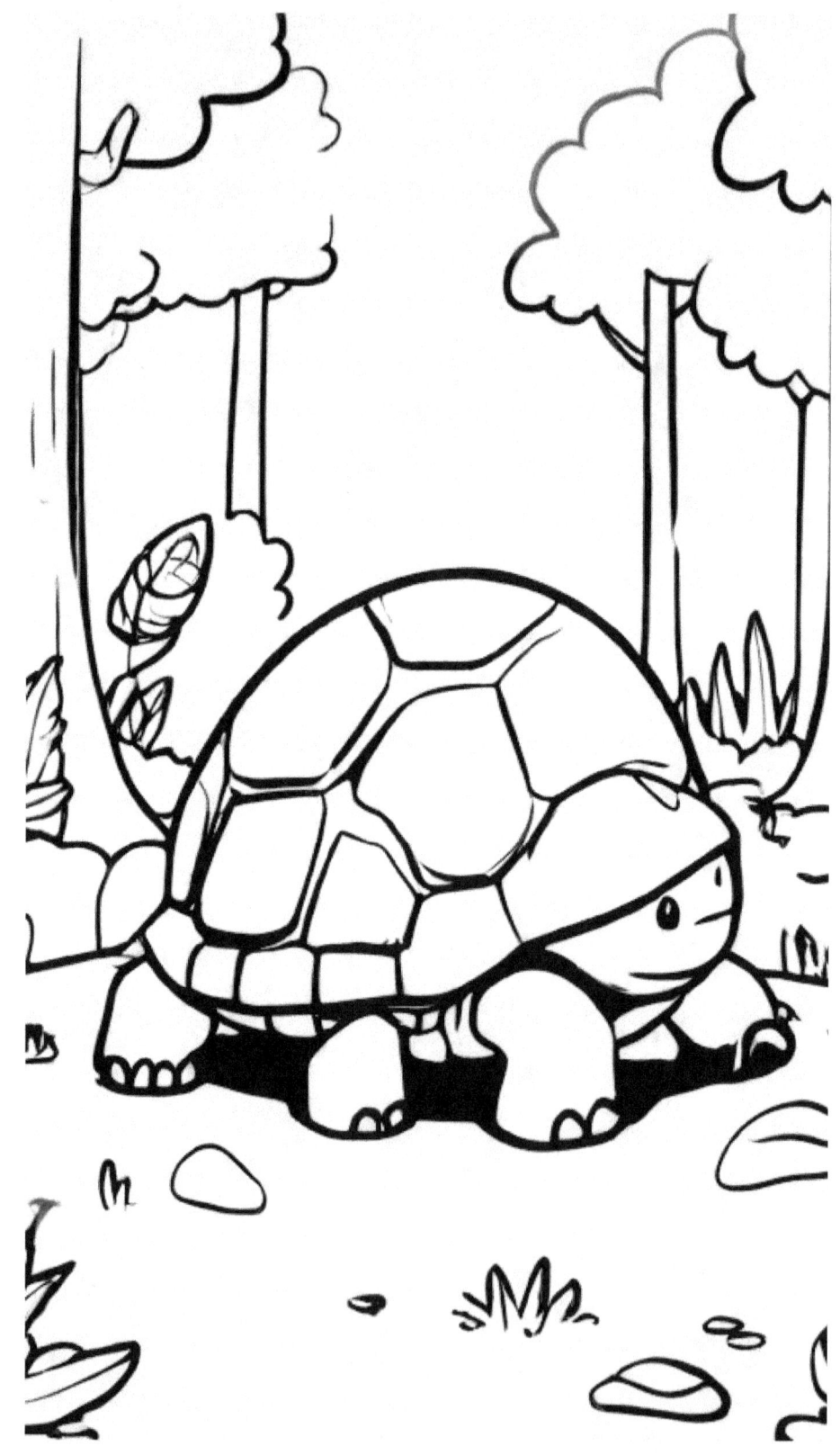

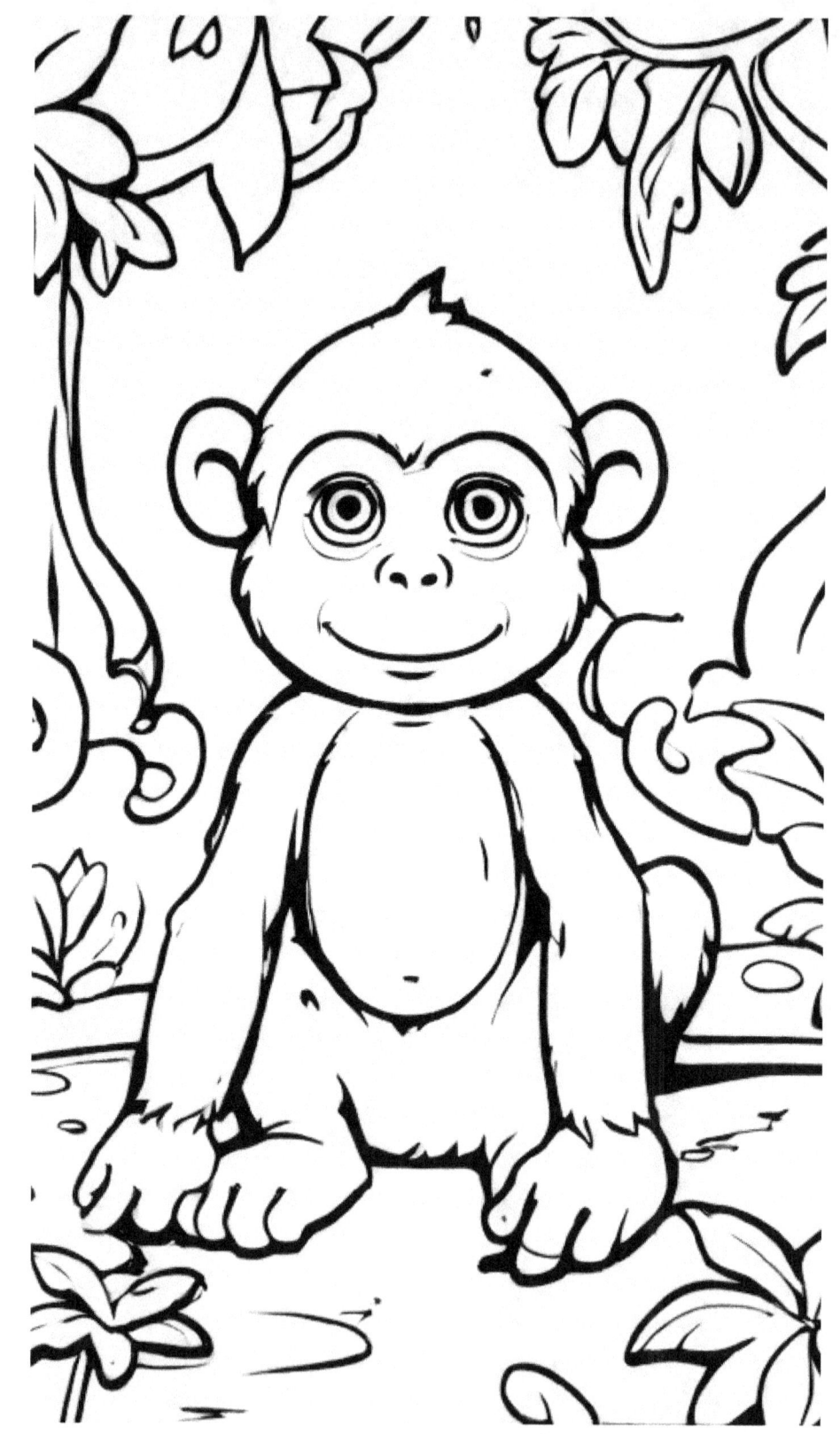

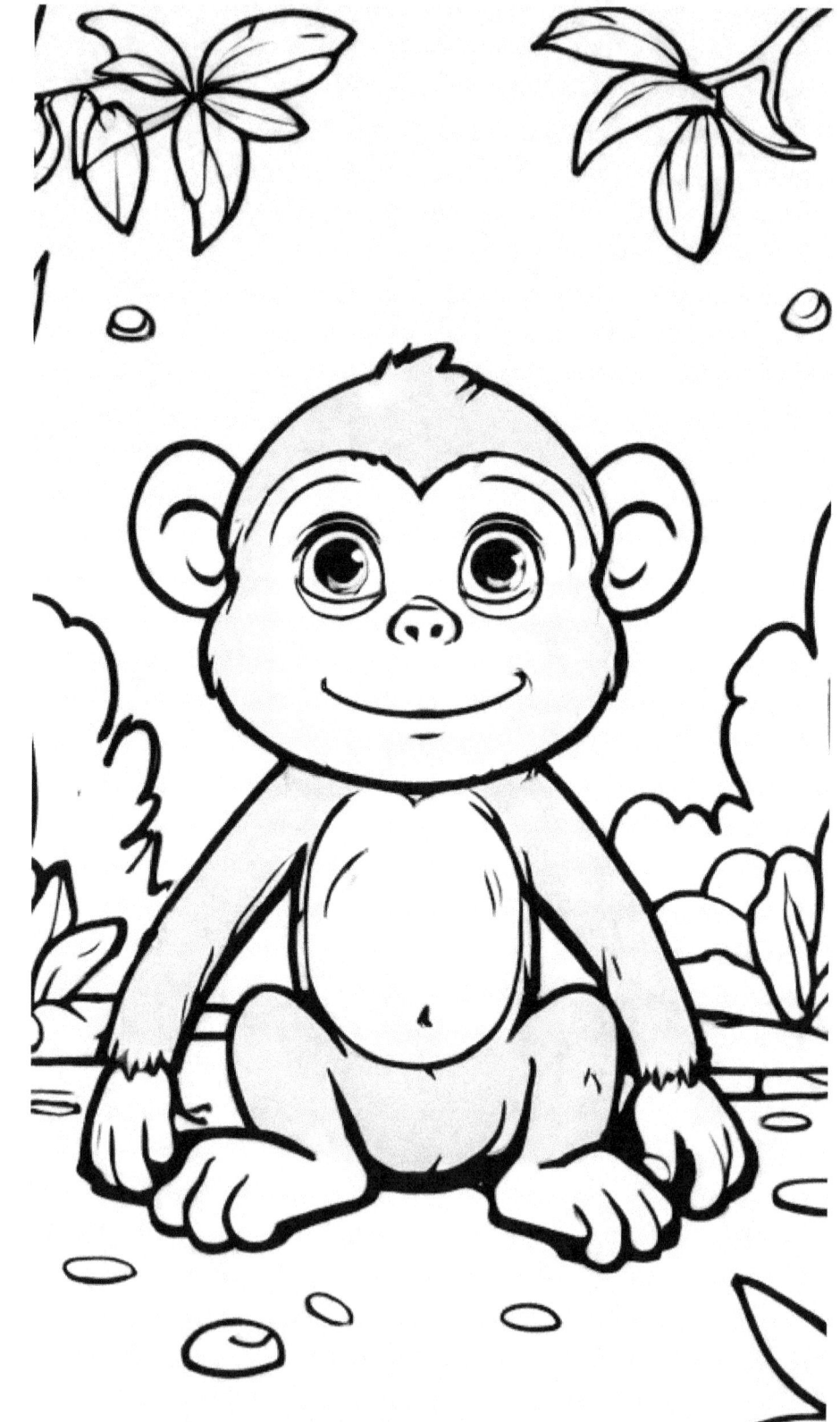

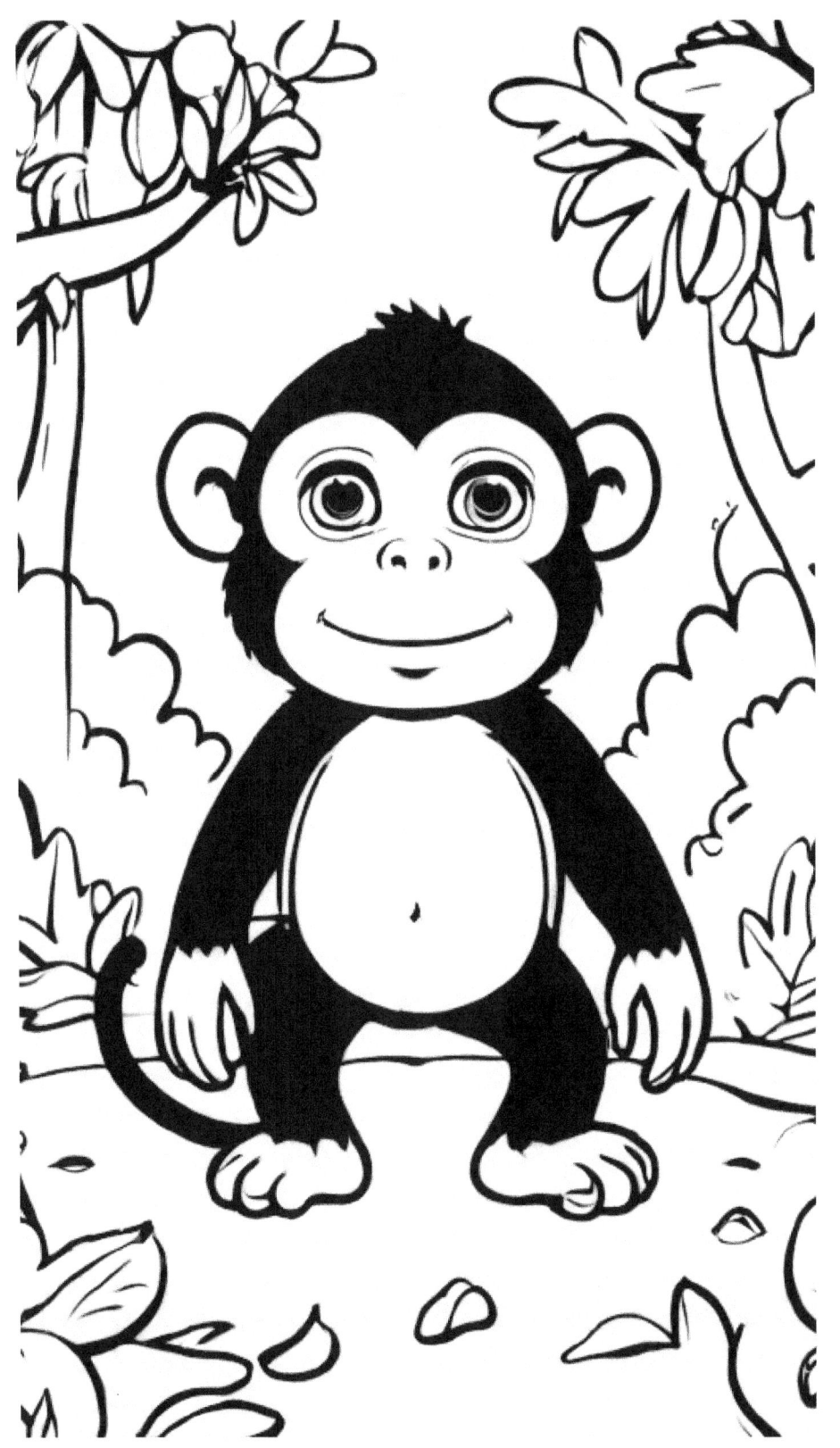

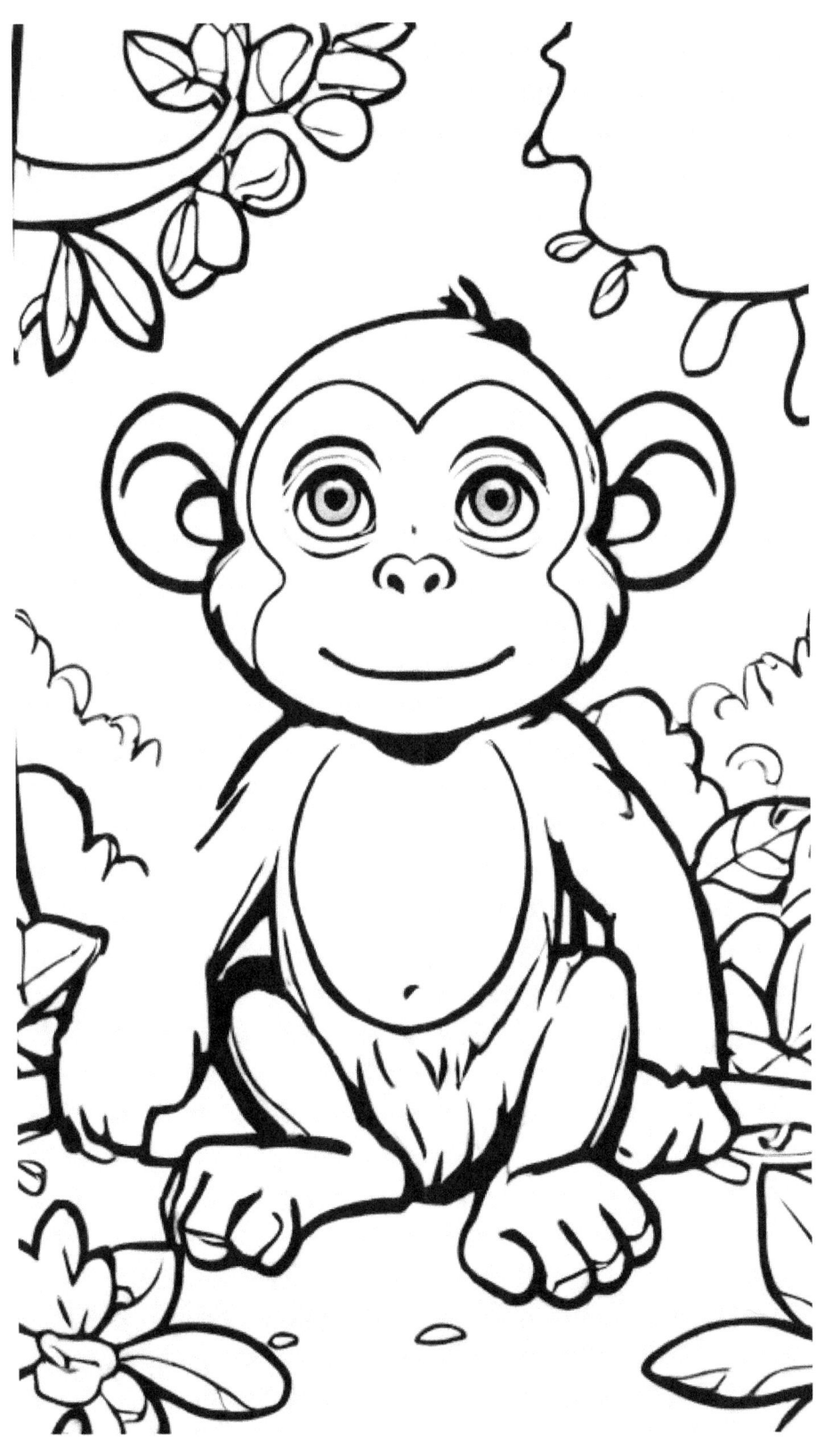

www.ingramcontent.com/pod-product-compliance
Lightning Source LLC
Chambersburg PA
CBHW071000290526
45795CB00005B/1718